Propose
LIKE A
MAN

©2013 Bob Woolsey
7705 N. Grand Prairie Drive
Peoria, IL 61615

ISBN 10: 0615816851
ISBN 13: 978-0615816852

Copyediting services by Chris Maddock

Proofreading services by Carl Nellis

Book design, typesetting and illustrations by Rusty Kinnunen,
www.rustyandingrid.com

Propose

LIKE A

MAN

BOB WOOLSEY

Edited by Chris Maddock

with illustrations by
RUSTY KINNUNEN

CONTENTS

LIST OF ILLUSTRATIONS

"You ever think about stuff?"
"Totally."
"Me too."

INTRODUCTION

You love the girl. For all your reckoning, she loves you back. And you want her to be your wife. Now all you have to do is propose.

Pretty simple, right?

It could be. But it probably shouldn't be. Because if you're like most guys, you haven't given a proposal of marriage a whole heck of a lot of thought. But believe me, you need to. And even if you have thought the whole thing out, you should probably noodle on the hows the wheres and the whens a bit more, just to make sure you're doing things the "best right way."

I say "best right way" because there really isn't an exact formula for coming up with and executing the perfect marriage proposal. That's not what this book is about. That would be ludicrous. I'm not going to give you a list of the "top ten" methods of marriage proposal—although I will share a number of awesome proposal stories. Likewise, other than not thinking through the thing at all, I won't advise you against any specific proposal ideas—although I will let you in on some of the most disastrous proposals I've ever heard. They're sad and awful and hilarious and teach profound lessons. And I've heard a lot of them.

This book isn't about pre- or post-marriage counseling, either. People are funny. Put two of them together and the possibilities are endless—for good and bad. But I can tell you this: how you propose matters. It matters because of the way she is and how she thinks. It matters because you'll both remember the moment as well as anything you'll ever do or see. Think about that.

This book is about preparing you for one of the most

important actions you'll ever take (whether you know it to be or not yet), giving you insight to help you determine your own "best right way," and taking you through some of the important details, like buying a ring and capturing the big moment for perpetuity. This book is about getting you to view your proposal with the proper respect so that it will be right, and perfectly memorable, and as exciting as anything you'll ever do.

In these pages, my intention is to show you:

◊ the importance of proposing with confidence, and how to make sure that happens

◊ how to find the right place to buy the ring

◊ how to buy the right diamond and engagement ring

◊ how to plan a unique, surprising, memorable proposal

So perhaps you're asking, "who's this guy who knows so much about proposing marriage that he feels he needs to write a book on the subject? Who made him expert?" Well, I did. Because for the last two decades I've been a part of the marriage of over twenty-five hundred couples. I've heard countless stories, innumerable concerns, fears and hopes, and most importantly, seen the outcomes of these proposals, often years after a marriage. That's what makes me an expert.

See, I'm a jeweler (maybe you thought I was a priest?). And as someone who chiefly sells engagement rings for a living, I get to see guys like you, right where you are, every waking day. But this book isn't about me. Actually that's a lie—for the next few pages it will be.

Home Run

A couple came into the store not long ago with a crazy story. Both Kori and Alyson worked for our local Single A baseball squad—The Peoria Chiefs. One day Kori decided he'd make his first move, so he tossed Alyson a baseball with a note attached asking for her phone number. It worked and they started dating. After a time, when Kori decided it was time to make his next big move, he stuck with what worked the first time. As he and Alyson were playing catch in the backyard, Kori rolled that same first-date ball to her with another note attached. This one read, "will you marry me?"

The Takeaway: it's romantic and meaningful to remember your first date. If you propose the right way, she'll feel the same way about your proposal.

MIA

I met Mia in 1997. We were leaders on a youth retreat weekend. She came to work at our family jewelry store and knew that at some point I would recognize her as the one. But it wasn't until that one warm August night that I really knew I was done for. We met with friends at a bar on the riverfront and when I saw her I knew something was different. We were meant to be together forever. We had to. Sure, it was magic and all of that. There were fireworks to be certain. But mainly it was like I was on cruise control. Like after years of driving in crazy, Mexico City traffic, all of the sudden I hopped onto the rails and didn't have to steer. It just went. I'm serious. As soon as I dropped her off for the evening, I said, "Yep, Mia's the one."

So there I was, in the situation I set up at the beginning of this book. I loved the girl. For all my reckoning, she loved me. And all I had to do now was propose.

But by this time, I had sold engagement rings to hundreds of guys. I'd asked them how they were going to propose. I'd listened to hundreds of them, and just as importantly, thousands of couples together. I'm not Freud by a long shot, but given that many years of exposure, it would be hard for anyone not to get a pretty good idea of what mattered, what worked, what didn't, and why—which is the reason I'm telling you about my own engagement.

I love and revere the mountains. Many of my most special moments have happened there. When I knew I was going to propose to Mia, I immediately knew I wanted to do so in the mountains. Over the years, I came to the conclusion that **one of the more important factors in a successful, beautiful and positively remembered proposal was that it be treated with special significance; with a sort of reverence and circumstance.** This may seem obvious to most, but the "why" bears explaining.

I can picture a lot of women who have excitedly told me otherwise, but I'm sure of it: **your bride-to-be wants the fairy tale.** If she tells you otherwise, don't believe her. Just don't. For whatever reason—personal, cultural or biological, **your gal has imagined being proposed to since she was a little girl. You need to remember that.**

By the time we left for the mountains, where I was going to propose, Mia and I had been together for about 8 months. Luckily, I had fibbed and told Mia that I would never, ever propose to anyone until we had been dating for a full year. Which was awesome. It meant **I had another key to a powerful,**

properly memorable proposal in my favor: the element of surprise. While Mia knew I loved the mountains, and knew that a trip like the one we were about to take would be a likely moment for a proposal—she wasn't expecting it this soon.

"So...do you want kids someday?"

You would think that a jeweler by trade would have an easy time with the whole ring part of the proposal. You'd be right. **But another thing I've learned over the years: the ring shouldn't give any guy pause. That part should be a slam dunk, no matter who you are, or what you can afford to spend on a ring.** As I'll explain later in the book, if this is a gal worth marrying, she's gonna love you no matter what ring you give her—as long as you pull off a worthy proposal. That's what matters. And that's the point of this book.

So I brought my ring with me to the Vail ski resort, and was perfectly prepared to hatch my golden proposal scheme. The day before the engagement Mia blew every ligament in her knee out and was on crutches. This put a little kink in the plan. The next afternoon we were lucky enough to get a gondola to ourselves to ride to the top. Somewhere during that eight-minute ride, I summoned the needed courage, dropped knee ward, asked Mia to marry me, and by the time the doors opened at the top, she said she'd be my wife.

And that was perfect, because right there at the top, there just happened to be one of those professional on-mountain photographers always on hand to capture special moments with friends and family. Perfect! The pictures he took that day are some of our most prized possessions. They're sublime. Not necessarily in their detail or composition, but just that they were taken, then, right when it happened. Right when it mattered. Every time I walk down my hallway and see those pictures, knowing that Mia sees them too, I'm grateful that I thought through things enough to make sure they'd happen in the "best right way." In the pages to come, **I'll talk more about why it's so important to properly capture the moments during or around your proposal.**

Man, I'm probably not telling you anything you don't already know, but you've got to admit that asking a girl to marry you can be pretty heavy—as it should be. All I'm saying, is that I think I can help you through the whole thing.

So there it is: how you propose matters. It matters to her, and in the years to come, it will matter to you. The balance of this book is intended to help you make the most of this most important moment. To make sure you give your proposal the thought it deserves. But just as important, to have as much fun together and to experience as much joy and happiness as possible, because in my mind . . . that's what it's all about.

Taken for a Ride

So a guy in Iowa goes to the state fair the day before he plans to propose. He pays off the double Ferris Wheel operator to get him to go along with his scheme. He tells the operator that the next day he'll be wearing a bright orange shirt, and asks him to stop the wheel once he's at the very top. Of course, that's where he popped the question. She was most impressed. **The Takeaway: don't be afraid to grease some palms to make sure your plan comes off without a hitch.**

"You wanna maybe go back to my pad and, you know ... watch some movies or something."

CHAPTER 1

Engagement Ring and Proposal Intel — Becoming the Perfect Spy

This chapter is about using your inner sleuth to decide what type of ring, diamond and proposal she would prefer. Like much of my advice in this book, the longer you have to figure all of this out, the more likely you'll blow her away with the ring and a proposal, without giving away all of the surprise.

This chapter will show you:

◊ the importance of working ahead and giving yourself time to plan

◊ the information you need to gather to buy the right ring

◊ the information you need to begin to plan your "best right" proposal

◊ how to get all that information without blowing the surprise

And that's the crux—at least one of them—of a well-executed proposal. To the best of your ability, you want to give her the ring she's been dreaming about, in a way that's appealing to both of you. Of course you also want your proposal to be a surprise. That may seem like a tough balancing act.

I think you're up for it.

STARTING EARLY IS KEY. As soon as you know that she's the one and that you are going to propose to her, it's time to get to the necessary spy-work. You're after answers to questions both big and small. You're looking to find out everything from her ring size to whether or not she'll marry you. A playful, off-the-cuff trip to a jewelry store is a great place to start.

When I tell guys that they ought to bring their girlfriends into a jewelry store to gain needed intelligence, most worry they'll ruin the surprise. But keep this in mind: if she's the one and feels the same way as you do, her female intuition is probably telling her that a proposal is at least on the horizon. She'll feel it in the works. Your chances of completely and utterly fooling her are slim. And you probably don't want her in a state of complete shock, anyway. In my opinion, things happen most smoothly when she's thought about you proposing, and has seen herself accepting that proposal.

In light of that, a trip to a jewelry store to find out your respective ring sizes, and to dream together about what sort of ring she would want "if Mr. Right were to come along," can serve dual purposes. It will give you some of the important details you need to get her a dreamy ring, and it can actually serve to heighten her anticipation and attachment to you. Remember: while you're trying to figure out if she'd say "yes" if you ask, she's trying just as hard to figure out if you're going to ask at all. A trip to a jewelry store, far enough in advance, and some questions regarding her dream proposal, framed in the right way, can actually serve to reassure the both of you, so that the actual delivery and acceptance of your proposal can be made with maximum confidence and clarity. The actual proposal can still be a surprise; both in the way you do it, and where and when you do it.

Here's a list of some of the things you're trying to figure out in advance without ruining the ultimate surprise:

<u>Her ring size.</u> This is key. When you propose, the ideal outcome is that she says "yes," quickly followed by you slipping the ring about her finger. Obviously, knowing her ring size is key. This can easily be accomplished by an early trip to a jewelry store, where you can gain other valuable intelligence, as well.

<u>Her preferred ring style, precious metal and diamond shape of choice.</u> You may not know much about engagement rings or diamond shapes, but she more than likely does. No matter what you're going to spend on her ring, you'll have these choices to make. Obviously, the more detailed your knowledge of her ring preferences, the more perfect the moment will be for the both of you. You can gain insight into such preferences by gently talking to her friends and family, and inquiring here and there as to her tastes. And, of course, an early trip together to a

jewelry store can answer a lot of questions—for the both of you. If at all possible, and this requires some inner James Bond, try to get a few pictures of some of the styles and colors she likes. The camera on your phone makes this way easier than it was back in the old days, and will save you from having to fumble for a description at the jewelry store. One other great way to get a solid idea of her ring preferences: try to slyly get her to post a few pictures of rings she likes on a site like Pinterest or Facebook—so you can share it with someone at a jewelry store when needed. A picture trumps your description any day.

How she feels about certain modes of proposing. If possible, you want to figure out if she'd find a jumbotron marriage proposal more or less meaningful and romantic than one offered over a quiet dinner. Learn where some of her favorite places are and why they're meaningful to her. Identify her favorite food. To craft the perfect proposal you need to do your homework, and the subject is her. Hopefully, in the course of your relationship, you've already learned a lot of this stuff. If you haven't, you should. Your deep interest in her is never a bad thing, and it just might reveal the secret to creating a world-class proposal.

The Old Switcheroo

What do you do when your gal knows you're about to propose? When she even knows when you're going to propose? I heard about a guy who told his girlfriend they were going to Las Vegas for a long weekend. She knew it was on. Only she didn't really know where. When they got to the airport, he walked her to a gate that said, "Paris, France." Yeah, she knew he was going to propose but she couldn't have dreamed it would happen in Paris. The lesson? If possible, propose in Paris.

"What about our house?"
"They told me to spend two month's salary."

CHAPTER 2

How Much Should You Spend on Her Engagement Ring?

Remember those commercials that used to advise you to spend two months' salary on the engagement ring you buy your fiancé? For the life of me, even as a jeweler who's been in the business of selling engagement rings for a very long time, I can't quite figure out the true intention behind those ads.

On the one hand, I can see value in getting guys to understand that spending enough to make it pinch a bit will probably insure that she'll be happy with the value he places on her.

I get that. On the other hand, two months' salary can be such a faulty gauge of what a guy should really spend that sometimes I believe it was just a marketing ploy to get guys to spend a lot of money on engagement rings. Who knows?

At any rate, what you should spend on her engagement ring is an entirely personal thing, and will come from a complicated mix of what is possible to spend, reasonable for you, and what she knows you can afford and what will make her feel valued and special.

As I mentioned earlier in the book, if she's worth marrying, she'll likely say "yes" to your proposal and love the ring no matter what you spend. On the flip side of the coin, if you're worth marrying, she might be thinking you should spend a touch more than is perfectly easy or comfortable—because she's worth it.

That sort of "it should hurt a little bit" amount may seem like a pretty squishy and ambiguous figure. In general terms, yes, it is. But over the years I've found that couples who are close enough to consider marriage to one another, are usually pretty close in their conception of what that proper payout should be.

Let's put it plainly: your girl knows what you make, how you live, and what things cost. What's important to her, even if unsaid and not specifically considered, is that your purchase of her engagement ring be significant and meaningful to you. It should hurt a little bit. It should be, to some degree, a sacrifice.

That said, my job is to help you understand how much money you'll be able to spend when you do purchase her engagement ring. You will also need to know if you'll need credit to get to your magic number.

See if this exercise can clarify things a little:

Calculate the amount of money you have in the bank or other reserves that you'll be able to use toward the purchase of her ring $_____.

After living expenses, and other necessary monthly expenditures, how much money can you save per month $_____ x number of months till you propose = $_____.

Add these amounts = $_____.

Is the amount you came out with less than what you feel you need to spend on her engagement ring? If so, can you get, and are you willing to use, credit to pay for the difference between what you can save and what you feel like you'd like to spend? Interest-free financing is available at most jewelry stores and can help it all work better for your wallet.

Doing this simple math should be helpful both in saving what you'll need to spend to make you both happy, and in getting you to further realize the significance of your proposal.

So how much should you spend on her engagement ring?

◊ enough to make her feel special and worth sacrificing for

◊ enough to make you feel confident in the ring you give

◊ enough to show that you value the moment, and enough to make you value the moment

Aim High

The Signature at the 95th is a nice restaurant near the top of Chicago's 2nd tallest building—the Hancock. It's not the swankiest spot in town by a long shot, but it is the highest place at which you can dine for about a thousand miles in any direction. A few years back, a client of mine took his unwitting girlfriend to the 95th floor restaurant, where he had bribed the wait staff to put the ring box on the desert plate. She saw the view, with Chicago's famously long, straight boulevards stretching to the west, and the black of Lake Michigan to the east, and said, "yes." **Takeaway: when it comes to proposing—it's hard to go wrong with a combination of elevation and dessert.**

"This is crazy. This is crazy. This is crazy."

CHAPTER 3

Where to Buy the Ring

As you might imagine from a jeweler like me, I do have opinions when it comes to where to buy her engagement ring. I think you should buy it at my store.

That's both completely true, and completely false. If you were in my area, and planned to live here, then I would, with certainty, tell you to buy her engagement ring at my store. If you live elsewhere, and that's where you're going to remain, then I'd recommend you buy your engagement ring and diamond from somewhere like my store.

The point: where you buy her engagement ring matters. It matters because she'll want and need to know where the ring and diamond came from. When she asks you, "where did you get the ring?" and you answer, "online," or "oh, just at the Mall or Wal-Mart or Costco or something," what are you really telling her? You're telling her that the most important factor in deciding where you bought her ring was price. And that's not a very romantic message. And please, please remember: this is one of the most important and long-lasting messages you'll ever communicate to her.

If you buy her a great ring, from a place you're proud of, there's an awful good chance the ring will become a valued part of your family history. If you respect this part of the process, you'll be adding an heirloom to the ones your father and grandfathers chose for the family. And that's pretty cool.

Bear in mind:

◊ You want the ring you give, and if possible, where it came from, to be a part of a story that you're proud of.

◊ Buying your ring from somewhere you're proud of, and possibly paying a touch extra than at some big chain place, a mall, or some price-club is well worth it. You'll be happy and confident in your choice, and as mentioned, your own confidence is key to a great proposal.

Where you buy her engagement ring will either become a valued and revered part of your personal history together, or it will become a regrettable and shameful little secret. Hey, I'm all for pinching pennies wherever I can. We all have to be smart. But believe me on this account: your proposal of marriage, and where the ring comes from, shouldn't be skimped on.

So here's the real skinny: you can save a little money buying a ring and a diamond online, at some big warehouse retailer, or in a seedy, big city jewelry district. But very little. So little that you'll probably end up paying more in short order by not getting the free maintenance and warranty services a good independent jewelry store will offer you with the purchase of a ring. And you'll be missing out on so much more.

If you vie for saving a tiny bit of money, you'll miss out on what, in many cases, becomes a lifetime relationship with a store and its people. You miss out on the confidence that comes from knowing you have a reputable company standing behind your ring. Don't think that matters? It does. I have couples who love to come in to talk to the salesperson who helped with the ring and the proposal. These salespeople and the stores they represent often become important parts of well-remembered proposal stories. And over time those stories becomes more and more valuable—worth far more than the pittance you might save by going the cheapest possible road. Heck, they sometimes even get invited to the wedding.

ASK YOURSELF: when you tell the story of how you proposed, will you be proud to talk about where you got the ring? Will you want to recommend the place to other couples? Will that place become part of your personal story or history, or is it something you'll want to cover up and hide?

Do you and your bride-to-be a big favor and buy your ring from a reputable independent jeweler in the town in which you live. Get to know the people there and let them help you make your proposal and your ring the best it can be.

In time, you'll thank me for this advice.

A Little Song 'n' Dance

You may have seen this one online. It went viral the moment someone posted it: Portland actor Isaac Lamb drives to the park with his girlfriend, Amy Frankel. He sits her in the open, back hatch of their SUV and nonchalantly tells her to put on some headphones and listen to a song. As the song begins to play, people begin to appear behind the car singing and dancing. First, Amy and Isaac's two best friends show up. Then more. Then dozens of people dancing in choreographed unison—all singing the song she's listening to in her headphones, asking her to marry Isaac, who at the very end of the song appears behind the crowd of dancers dressed formally carrying a ring. **The Takeaway: Amy said all the work Isaac put into the proposal was "good insurance" she'd say yes. I'd say so.**

"Oh, Teddy—I do!"
"But..."

CHAPTER 4

Buying the Ring

If you're like most guys, and not a jeweler like me, you know as much about engagement rings as a dachshund knows about deep-sea exploration. Actually, that's not true. If you've followed my advice up to this point in the book, you know way more than that wiener.

You know:

◊ if you're going to surprise her with a simple ring and, thus, spend most of your time shopping for the diamond.

◊ if she knows about your impending proposal and wants to shop for her ring and diamond with you. This changes a lot. For instance, you really don't have to worry about performing any more pre-purchase intelligence.

◊ about how much you can spend on the ring.

◊ that you should probably buy the ring from a reputable jeweler, even if you have to spend a few extra dollars.

◊ that you need to do some further reconnaissance in order to assess her ring style preferences and that doing so well in advance can afford you important information while still retaining the element of surprise.

If you know all that stuff, congrats, you're miles ahead of most guys. You're well on your way to not flubbing the ring portion of your proposal. For all my talk about how if she's worth marrying, she won't care what you give her, a great ring will help in both the moment of proposal and in the years to come. Noodle on it: there are really only 4 major elements of the proposal: you, the ask, the scene and the ring. And the ring is the only one of those that she'll attach to her body for the rest of her life. Note I said "rest of her life."

Just a Kiss

I was eating at a restaurant when the server told me her proposal story. It was Christmas and she was at the home of her boyfriend's parents. After opening gifts and eating, his Mom announced that it was "time to hang the mistletoe," and that she wanted to get some pictures of all the kids and their significant others under it. Little did my server know that her boyfriend and his Mom were in cahoots and up to something sneaky. When their turn came to pose under the mistletoe, as the pictures were popping and the video rolling, he asked her to marry him right there in front of the family. **The Takeaway: as long as she likes your family, nothing shows you want her to be a part of your life like proposing in front of the family.**

"I was wondering... can I see a picture of your mother?"

So if I were you, I'd aim higher than "not flubbing" and try to hit this part of the proposal out of the park. The chapter is intended to help you accomplish just that—to buy her a ring you're confident she'll like. The elimination of her possible disappointment with the ring, and the confidence that will inspire, will transfer to your ask, and that will make everything go more smoothly and ultimately result in a cooler, more valuable memory. And grasshopper—that is the whole idea.

If, in your ring-recon (hopefully accomplished some time before you're ready to shop for the thing) you've found out that she wants a specific ring made by a specific designer, then your

job has become much easier. If you can afford to get her such
a ring, then you really have no sane choice but to buy it. If
that's the case, then you should just flip ahead a few pages to the
next section on buying the diamond. Because once you have the
right ring—that's all you need. I'd give the same advice if you
want to completely surprise your baby. In such a case, I'd advise
buying a simple "solitaire mounting" and concentrate your ef-
forts on searching for the best diamond in your budget. Some
gals are fine with this old-school, simple type of ring. But not
most. Not these days.

If you do surprise your sun 'n' moon with a solitaire mount,
and know she'll probably prefer something different later, then
let her know that this is an option. Tell her so after you propose
(and she accepts, of course). She'll appreciate the surprise, AND
that you know her well enough to know she'd like to choose her
own ring style.

More women actively shop for their own engagement ring
than ever before. A lot more. I think part of this is a result of
so many couples living together far in advance of their engagement. Part of it is the exposure that women have the many im-
ages of designer jewelry available in magazines and on the web.
Whatever the reason, most women accompany their men to the
jewelry stores, having already been proposed to, or well aware
that a proposal is forthcoming. And for whatever reason—maybe they don't trust their guy to pick out the right ring, or they're
just finicky and know what they want—these gals feel the need
to be an active part of the shopping process.

INSIDERS TIP: even if you're about to go "active shopping" with a gal who knows you're going to propose, don't be
fooled into thinking she doesn't still want the romance and
surprise of a great proposal.

I use the phrase "active shopping" to differentiate this type of couples shopping from a guy who has playfully prodded his sweetie into a jewelry store to gain insight into her preferences. In the second scenario, the gal is most often uncertain of a guy's intentions. In an active shopping situation, she's usually well aware of what's happening.

In fact, if your proposal isn't a secret, or even if you've already proposed, I tell guys to treat shopping for and purchasing her engagement ring as if the whole enterprise is a surprise. Think about it: you'll get another chance to gain Don Juan points, and she gets to live the dream like she's imagined it since she was a little girl.

INSIDERS TIP: if you communicate with the jewelry store about her engagement ring—do it via email, and not text. You don't want a spoiler from a sales rep telling you "the ring is ready" popping up on your phone and ruining the surprise.

The lesson? Don't buy her ring while she's with you. Optimally, she'll give you a few options of what she likes. That way you won't just surprise her with your proposal, you'll surprise her with what ring you've chosen. This also gives you some room to maneuver financially so you can get her a ring you know she'll like, at a price that you can afford.

What a View

A friend of mine recently went on a hike up on a cliff above Poipu in Kauaii with his longtime girlfriend, whom he blindfolded toward the end of the hike. She obviously knew something was afoot. When they reached the top, looking out on an amazing view of the ocean, he removed the blindfold and

proposed. What she didn't know, but soon real-
ized, was that gathered behind them were each
of their families. She had no idea they were there
until she had already said yes. **The Takeaway: you
can make great things even better with a little
plotting and scheming.**

Shopping Without Her

M ost guys who come shopping for an engagement ring ar-
en't aware of a specific designer choice, and often arrive
able only to rough out a mental sketch of style and color and the
like. That's OK. Most good jewelers can help. They're sort of like
the sketch artists employed by the cops. With a little time devot-
ed to listening to your mumbles, they can usually come up with
a good rendering of what your girl will like.

Or, if you follow my advice from earlier in the book, you'll
procure a picture or two of style choices during an early, playful trip to the jewelry store. Yes, this requires some stealth. But
doing so will ease your shopping experience and mitigate the
risk of buying something she wouldn't wear to a costume party.
If you have pictures, things get simple: bring these to the jewelry store, find a nice salesperson, and point to the pictures. If
the jeweler is worth their salt, they'll return in moments with a
number of options in no time.

**SUPER INSIDERS TIP: want to know the real skinny?
I'll tell you, even though this may make some of my jeweler
friends a little uneasy. If you can use your ring-intel pictures
to locate similar rings online—and you probably can—have
that ring at the most competitive price displayed on your
phone and show it to the jeweler. Without saying a word, and**

without having to haggle or fuss, the salesperson will recognize that you've done your homework. All stores have some wiggle room on rings, and an actual quoted price WILL get them to wiggle.

BONUS POINTS: if you've done good detective work, and you know the style of ring she prefers, there are two things you can do to make the ring, the proposal you make with it, and the stories about it in the future, more special:

Find a store that sells her preferred ring style. Ask them how long it would take the manufacturer to send you a brand new ring. If you have the time to spare, her appreciation of this "virgin" ring will be well worth the extra effort.

If you really want to make it over-the-top special, and you have the time and money, find a store that does custom work to create a one-of-a-kind creation in her preferred style. Nothing is more romantic than this, but you should be very confident that you know what she wants if you go this route.

I'll reiterate this at the end of the next chapter, but since it bears repeating, I'll say it first here: it never hurts to ask for a better price. As mentioned, almost all stores have wiggle room built into their pricing—both on ring mountings and on diamonds. But they won't wiggle unless you clearly demonstrate that you've done your homework, or you ask them to. So don't be afraid to ask for a better price. You just might get it.

Avoid the Mall at All Costs

While writing this book a buddy told me about a video he saw online. I found it. It shows a man in a suit proposing at the food court in a mall. You could almost forgive the guy (the girl is pretty cute) if the proposal was spontaneous. It wasn't. Halfway into the video a guitar guy comes into frame serenading the couple with a rendition of "Sweet Caroline."

The Takeaway: Caroline wasn't so sweet. At least not on a guy who decided to propose at the mall food court. At the end of the video you see "Caroline" speed away. Ouch.

"Are you wearing cologne?"
"No, uh ... it's probably just my deodorant."

CHAPTER 5

The Rock

Chicks love diamonds. Why they're mesmerized so much by this sparkly carbon is Greek to most males. So what. She loves them. And as you'll learn in the years to come, such reliable and specific insight into how she works and what she likes is rare. It should be celebrated and taken advantage of. There's no more important time to do so than in your proposal.

In this chapter, we'll cover:

◊ how to research diamonds

◊ how to use diamond certificates to your benefit

◊ the importance of seeing and buying a diamond in person

◊ how to get the best diamond at your budgeted price

You alone know how much you can spend on her engagement ring and diamond. The real question: how do you get the most diamond for your money? The answer: more homework.

The whole world of jewelry, jewelry stores, and diamonds has changed completely in the last ten years. And that's a good thing for the layman about to buy a diamond. Before the internet and big diamond websites like Blue Nile, you had to do a lot of real looking and legwork to get a true idea of the going prices of different qualities of diamonds. Today you can obviously do most of your research online, and then shop well fortified with the knowledge to get the most for your money.

Color	Carat | Weight	Clarity	Cut
Colorless D E F	0.25	FL / IF	Emerald
Near Colorless G H I J	0.50	VVS₁ / VVS₂	Heart
Faint K L M	1.00 1.25	VS₁ / VS₂	Marquis
Very Light N O P Q R	1.50 1.75	SI₁ / SI₂	Oval
Light S T	2.00 2.50	I₁ I₂	Pear
Yellow U V	3.00	I₃	Princess Round

THE FOUR C's

Spend a good amount of time on diamond websites like BlueNile.com and Brilliance.com searching for diamonds in your price range. Along the way, you'll read a good deal about the 4 C's—color, cut, clarity and carat weight—the common reference points shared by jewelers and gemologists used to determine relative diamond value.

Read up on the 4 C's. Understand what they mean. Look for diamonds online in your price range. Know what happens to price when you get to the most colorless of the color ratings, and where a slight concession in naked-eye clarity will result in a big reduction in price. Print out the descriptions of a few good quality diamonds in your price range, with the prices apparent and legible on-page. You'll need these.

Then, when you're really well schooled in the art and science of diamonds online—don't buy online. If I have one rule of broken-thumb I'll shout to the world, it's this: whatever you do, don't buy your diamond online. As you'll see when you move your study from the online world to real stores and real diamonds, individual diamonds have qualities you and she will notice that aren't defined by grades or rating systems. If you buy online you'll never see these very personal, often amazingly beautiful differences in diamonds of exactly the same "graded" quality and price. Not to wax too woo woo here, but sort of like her, the right diamond will speak to you. And that can only happen up-close and in person.

To the Stores

Most guys buy their ring mounting and diamond from the same store. And as long as you like and respect a particular jeweler, sometimes doing so has advantages. For one, the warranty on your ring and your diamond will be with the same company. And you can often get a store to make you an exceptional deal on a ring+diamond package compared to the cost

GIA
GEM TRADE LABORATORY

DIAMOND GRADING REPORT
DATE:

| | GIA CLARITY SCALE | GIA COLOR SCALE | GIA CUT SCALE |

Laser Inscription Registry........................**GIA XXXXXXXXXX**
Shape and Cutting Style........................**ROUND BRILLIANT**
Measurements ....6.62 - 6.68 x 4.03 mm

GRADING RESULTS - GIA 4Cs

Carat Weight ....**1.09 carat**
Color Grade ....**I**
Clarity Grade **SI2**
Cut Grade ....**Excellent**

ADDITIONAL GRADING INFORMATION

Finish
   Polish ....Excellent
   Symmetry........................Excellent
Fluorescence ....None
Comments:
Clouds are not shown.
Pinpoints are not shown.

FLAWLESS
INTERNALLY FLAWLESS
VVS₁
VVS₂
VS₁
VS₂
SI₁
SI₂
I₁
I₂
I₃

D E F G H I J K L M N O P Q R S T U V W X Y Z

EXCELLENT
VERY GOOD
GOOD
FAIR
POOR

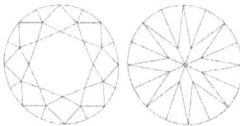

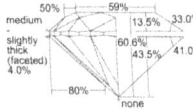

Key to Symbols

50% | 59%
medium | 13.5% | 33.0°
slightly thick (faceted) 4.0% | 60.6% | 43.5% | 41.0°
80%
none

Profile to actual proportions

PRICE: $5,500.00

A GIA certificate is usually more accurate and will display a higher price than an EGL certificate, but the GIA diamond will usually be more attractive to the naked eye.

DIAMOND CERTIFICATE
issued by the

EGL • USA
EUROPEAN GEMOLOGICAL LABORATORY™

Natural Diamond Report

Certificate	US00000000D
WEIGHT	1.09 CT
Shape and cut	ROUND BRILLIANT
Measurements	6.62 - 6.68 x 4.03 mm
PROPORTIONS	
Depth:	60.6%
Table:	59%
Crown:	13.5%
Pavilion:	43.5%
Girdle	MEDIUM TO SLIGHTLY THICK FACETED
Culet:	NONE
FINISH	
Polish:	EXCELLENT
Symmetry:	EXCELLENT
CLARITY GRADE	SI2
COLOR GRADE	I
Flourescence:	NONE
Comments:	Clouds are not shown.
	Pinpoints are not shown
DATE:	

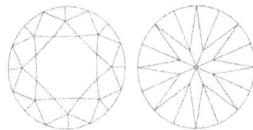

EUROPEAN GEMOLOGICAL LABORATORY™
EGL USA

PRICE: $3,900.00

*An EGL certificate is usually less accurate and will display a
lower price than a GIA certificate, but the EGL diamond will
usually be less attractive to the naked eye.*

of buying them separately. On the other hand, if you can't get a great deal on both, and you like the people and the deals you find on a diamond elsewhere, by all means, take your business elsewhere.

Find a jeweler you like and trust. Find a jeweler that's dedicated to getting you a diamond that speaks to you that YOU see value and beauty in, even if the jeweler has to bring diamonds in on memo from vendors. When you're out hunting diamonds in the real world, ask to use a jewelers "loupe" or microscope. Get accustomed to finding the imperfections with the loupe, and how they affect the overall look of the diamond when you're not looking through it. A lot of guys find the best value in their price range buying a diamond with imperfections identifiable under magnification, that are nevertheless invisible to the naked eye.

When shopping your chosen store or stores, bring printed copies of the certificates and prices for diamonds priced competitively online in your price range. Take it or leave it type negotiating doesn't work well if you don't have a better price to leave for. Bringing printouts of diamonds online gives you strong negotiating ammunition from the get-go.

In general, avoid jewelers who can't find a diamond in your price range. Avoid jewelers who try to make you "understand" the value of something you can't see to justify a jump in price. Avoid jewelers who are pushy and that you don't trust. As I've mentioned—and this is sort of the zen of proposing—being confident that you've done all the right things and are doing the right thing will make the moment of proposal more powerful for both of you. If at all possible, get her a ring you're confident she'll appreciate. Propose in a manner that you're confident she'll remember fondly. Buy her a diamond you're confident she'll revere and in which she'll see the same beauty you did. And get it from a jeweler you like and feel confident has your back. Do all of those things in the "best right way," and you'll have a hard time not feeling the calm confidence from which strength emanates. And in that special moment, she wants you calm, confident, and strong. You've got this. Be the man. Propose like a man.

Choosing the One

As crazy as it sounds, choosing just the right diamond is more subjective than scientific. Once you know what you can spend and have options in the same size and quality range (something you should strive to have), choosing the perfect diamonds is a lot like falling in love. Don't settle on a diamond. No matter what you have to spend, don't buy a diamond until one speaks to you. I don't really know exactly how to say it, because it will be a personal thing, but you'll know the right diamond when you see it, and the reason it's "just the one" won't show up on a diamond's certificate.

That said, you should acquaint yourself with GIA and EGL diamond certificates, the common differences between their rating tendencies, and what those mean when it comes to choosing and paying for a your diamond.

In general, the GIA (Gemological Institute of America) grades diamonds more strictly than the EGL (European Gemological Laboratory). That means that two diamonds rated equally by the two agencies will usually vary to the eye of a highly trained gemologist. That highly trained professional will usually see the GIA diamond a grade higher in color, clarity, or both. This is meaningful. It generally means that "on paper" you'll get more diamond for less money when purchasing an EGL diamond compared to a GIA diamond. It means you should expect GIA certified diamonds to be somewhat more expensive than a similarly graded diamonds with EGL certificates. Of course, you could also expect to get more for GIA diamonds should you sell them.

And while you should get familiar with GIA and EGL certificates, don't get too caught up in them. They are not the end-all. Although most certificates vary slightly in how they grade diamonds, most all are acceptable verifications of a diamond's size, shape and general authenticity, as long as you're aware of their general grading tendencies and how that affects price.

Optimally, at the moment of truth, you'll have a bunch of diamonds at your price to choose from, with minor technical differences in some of the C's. At that point, you need to take off the loupe, step back and channel Luke Skywalker a bit. Use your force. Allow yourself the confidence to trust your eye. Then do it. Pick the one you like best.

There are just a few important details to look into before you hand over the credit card. First, find out who manufactures the ring and whether the store or the manufacturer warranties the ring. Find out if the store warranties the diamond. If two stores charge the same for a ring or a diamond, but one has a better warranty, then go with the better warranty. There's a store I know of in Wisconsin with the strongest diamond warranty on earth: if you lose the diamond, for whatever reason, they'll replace it, no questions asked. As you can imagine, this is the most popular place to buy an engagement ring in the area.

Likewise, ask each jeweler about their trade-up policy. Later in life, your gal may want a bigger diamond. And you may just want to buy her one. A 1-to-1 trade-in value policy has become much more common in the jewelry world, and should be your goal.

So get out there. Have fun. And do the homework necessary to confidently choose a killer diamond at a great price.

Fun in the Forest

I heard about a guy who shared the love of hunting for wild mushrooms with his gal. No, not those mushrooms. In fact, their biggest prize was the elusive "Morel" variety. One morning before hunting in a stretch of forest, the guy put a set of fabricated Mushrooms he had made with the ring in the middle along the trail they would take. There she found the engagement ring he had planted earlier. Wild 'shrooms, a girl in a forest—sounds like a fairy tale to me.

Of course she said yes.

CHAPTER 6

The Plan

The preceding chapters have hopefully given you some simple new tools and insights that you can use to find the right jewelry store and choose the right diamond and engagement ring. Now let's talk about your plan for the moment, and what things to build into it to ensure it's awesome, meaningful for the both of you, and well remembered.

I opened this book with the story of how I met my wife, Mia, and how I imagined, planned for and executed my proposal to her. I thought the story would be illustrative of the various components that go into creating a confident, well achieved proposal.

I also admitted that my years working as a jeweler and learning from thousands of guys and couples gave me something of an advantage. Of course it did. And that's why I wrote this book. To give you the same insight all those years have given me.

Where and how you propose matters because she'll remember that moment as well as anything she'll ever see or do. But that shouldn't give you the idea that coming up with a memorable proposal is necessarily difficult. It isn't. It's something that should be relatively easy to do as long as you remember to plan for a few, important things:

◊ plan far enough in advance so you have time to plot, scheme and implement your plan

◊ make sure you "plan" for your surprise proposal

◊ decide if you'll ask her parents for her hand

◊ ensure that your proposal has some degree of pomp and circumstance, reverence, magic or thoughtfulness

◊ make sure you have a plan for carrying and delivering the ring during your proposal

◊ have a way to capture your proposal or recent aftermath in pictures or video

◊ plan a celebration of some sort to take place after your proposal and her acceptance

There's no perfect time to propose, no magic hour. The "best right" time for you and her is far enough in the future that you can plan what needs planning and set in place the things you're going to do to make the night special. Planning the events of that evening well enough in advance will keep you from having to hope for a reservation at the right restaurant or feel nervous about who might be able to attend a secret, after-proposal party.

So give yourself some time. It will only make the surprise even better when it happens.

Gone with the Wind

A London floor-fitter named Lefkos Hajji put the $10,000 engagement ring he had just purchased inside of a helium balloon, thinking she'd pop the balloon -- and he'd pop the question. But as he left the balloon store, a strong gust of wind pulled the balloon from his hands and into the London sky. Hajji then spent the next two hours chasing the balloon in his car and unfortunately, failing. Evidently, he purchased another ring and proposed in a more down to earth manner, finally getting a "yes."

There's no perfect place to propose. Not even for the two of you. There are probably dozens of places that would work well and be special. The key is doing your homework and using what only you know about her to choose somewhere that will feel special and comfortable, where you'll also be able to capture the moment and celebrate.

You, like everyone else, have seen a scoreboard proposal at a basketball game, or heard a story about some guy proposing via blimp. Should you do something big like that? I dunno. Your girl might be blown away, say "yes," and forever tell stories of your audacity. Then again, you might end up getting a humiliating "no" like one guy recently received at a nationally televised basketball game. Ouch.

Only you know whether she's the type of gal who would appreciate such a proposal. If you know her well enough to consider marriage to her, then you'll know of several places and ways that would seem romantic, perfect, fun, or over the top. But no matter where or how you pop the question, whether it's over breakfast in bed, or on the jumbotron in Times Square, it should be a surprise.

While planning with an acute attention to detail may seem at odds with a "surprise," in actuality, proper planning can drastically reduce the chances that something unexpected will spoil it. So whatever your mode and method, make sure that you'll be able to use the space you need to propose, and that any other participants necessary are ready and schooled in your plan. Set up and manage your surprise. As dorky as it sounds, I even advise guys to make sure they have a way—often the right clothing—to conceal the ring up to the actual moment.

There was a time in this country when it was routine for a young man to ask a girl's father for her hand in marriage. While that tradition is certainly waning in popularity, I still think it's a great way to show respect to her and her family and to get off on the right foot.

Personally, I knew I needed to ask Mia's dad for her hand in marriage. But I waited too long so I had to blow by her parent's house on the way home from work the night before we left for Colorado. I called Larry and said we needed to talk . . . tonight! He was worried. Mia's mother, Kay, was there as well, and worried too. I told them I loved their daughter and wanted their blessing. Larry's first comment: "you know you get both dogs." When he'd had that covered he and Kay were elated and thankful that I had stopped by. When we called to tell them that Mia had hurt her knee, Kay thought we were joking. I had to grab the phone and tell her that Mia had hurt her knee and that NOTHING ELSE HAD HAPPENED.

Should you ask your gal's father or parents for their blessing?

If you think it's part of your "best right way" to ask the parents, you should. It can make all parties happier, can communicate immense amounts of respect, and truly is proper etiquette.

A great proposal should contain some degree of excitement and hooplah. Some sort of pomp and circumstance. Something out of the ordinary. For some guys and their gals, the surprise of the proposal is enough to produce the required excitement to make the thing special and memorable. I've known hundreds of guys who said their proposal was completely unexpected. A lot of these guys proposed over dinner. A couple of them got down on a knee while at the museum with a display of a favorite artist. Another guy I know proposed on a ride up a ski lift. If she really doesn't know it's coming, she will be surprised, and likely make a bit of a memorable scene. Sometimes in these moments, it's fun to have other people present, known or unknown, to react to and be part of the big moment.

With more couples shacking up together well before marriage is even a consideration, fewer gals than ever are completely unaware that a proposal is forthcoming. Most know its likely to happen, and many are able to use their uncanny feminine wiles to know right when it's coming. This is, of course, true of the some 50% of women who shop with their men for their engagement rings. They smell what's cooking. In these sorts of scenarios, where the ask is anticipated and expected, the ask itself probably won't be entirely earth-shaking. In these situations, how and where you ask need to provide an extra dose of excitement and drama.

Ask yourself and answer honestly: does she even suspect you're going to ask her to marry you? Is she hopeful but unsure that it will happen? Or is she pretty sure it's gonna happen soon? If she has no clue what's coming, it might be enough to make sure there are some people around to react to her freaking out. But if she knows for sure that the question is coming, you might want to call in the white horses and blimps, so to speak.

Tip of the day: **if possible, get some exercise a couple hours prior to proposing. This will help you to blow off some steam and go into the ask feeling calm and confident.**

When She Says "Yes"

S ome guys say proposing was sort of like watching the scene from above—as if it was an out-of-body experience. Other guys say it was like buying a movie ticket. They weren't nervous in the least. No matter what it feels like, believe me, it will be over in a flash. Just like that, all your planning and hoping will come to a head and be gone. Hopefully you'll watch as she cries and smiles and laughs in the aftermath of a plan well executed. And hopefully, you'll have the people or means necessary to capture the moment for perpetuity.

If there's a key part of creating a lasting and memorable proposal where most guys fail, it's failing to capture quality pictures or video of the moment or just thereafter. As you'll recall, part if the beauty of my on-mountain ask was the top-of-lift photographer I was lucky enough to have present. I'm so thankful for that. I've heard of some guys hiring a video crew to tape their proposal from afar, even miking the area up to record the audio. It may be enough to bring along a camera for photos or videos. It could be as simple as giving your camera to the waiter at the beginning of the night and tipping well so he's ready to get some good pictures. However you do it, make sure you capture it. Like I am every time I walk past the pictures of that day at Vail: you'll both be glad you did so.

Because Mia and I were on vacation with friends and family, I knew we had a built-in post proposal get together. This is another thing becoming more prevalent these days, as more couples cohabit long before marriage. More guys are planning proposal parties where a small group of friends and family celebrate.

Give yourself the time to plan. Use your knowledge of what she's all about to create the best right proposal for you both, making sure it's a surprise and includes the requisite celebration and flair. Now all you have to do is pull the trigger.

Anyone for a Frosty?

Sometimes hiding the ring for your sweetie works out gangbusters, like it did for the mushroom hunting couple. Other stories of hiding the engagement ring don't have such an "easy outcome." Take the story of Reed Harris, who proposed to his girlfriend, Kaitlin Whipple at the local Wendy's. See, she really loved those Frosties, and Reed decided he'd pop the engagement ring in one, so she'd happen upon it while enjoying her favorite frozen confection. Oops. Quickly, one of Kaitlin's friends dared her to chug her Frosty (what are the chances, right?), and before Reed could do anything, Kaitlin was wiping her chin and the engagement ring was on a journey to the center of her. She said, "yes"—two days later when the ring reemerged.

"Uh—so, you wanna, like, get married or something?"

CHAPTER 7

The Ask

This last chapter will be brief. Because if you've prepared well, asking is easy. And one of the coolest things you'll ever do. You'll never, ever feel like such a man as in that moment when you propose marriage. I promise you that.

Your perfect proposal will be different than anybody else's. But in general, as the moment approaches, make sure you review your plan and feel confident in it. As you bob between nervousness, joy, and anticipation—which you'll certainly do—focus and refocus on the plan you're going to execute, and the thought you've put into it.

If just asking on a whim or dropping to a knee at any random moment consistently produced a confidently executed and well-remembered proposal, I wouldn't have written this book. But it doesn't. As I've mentioned, the suave, calm, focused, confident man of her dreams thing comes most commonly from thoughtful, careful planning and knowing that you know. That's what launches a championship proposal. If you're confident in where you purchased the ring, and confident that you bought the right ring and the right diamond, confident that she'll appreciate the moment in which you'll ask, and confident you've set up all you need to capture and remember the moment, then all that confidence will be there when you arrive at the very doorstep of your destiny.

Yes, I actually wrote that. The doorstep of your destiny, brother. And she would be your queen. Yeah, I thought sentiments like that were pretty corny before I fell in love and considered asking a woman to be my partner for the balance of our lives on earth. By the time I reached the bottom of the ski lift upon which I would propose, I didn't anymore. And neither will you—however you ask—as long as it's in your "best right way."

As the very moment approaches, if you've planed well and done your last minute detail check, time will slow and all else will fall away, as it does for athletes in the all-or-nothing moments they've practiced and planned for all their lives.

Then, quickly, it will be time. Give yourself a moment to take a long look at her. Look her in the eyes. Know with all your heart and mind that this woman must be your wife.

Then ask her to do so.

Isn't Love Puzzling?

I read recently about a couple from Washington DC that made the news for one of the best proposal stories I've ever heard. Corey Newman proposed to girlfriend Marlow Epstien using the Sunday Washington Post, with a little help from the crossword writer there. He embedded clues for her hometown, her first and last name, and lastly, the word: WILLYOUMARRYME? Wow. That's what I'm talkin' about.

"What do we do now?"
"Whatever we want."

www.ingramcontent.com/pod-product-compliance
Lightning Source LLC
Chambersburg PA
CBHW060617030426
42337CB00018B/3095